HIP-HOP

Snoop Dogg

Emma Carlson-Berne

Mason Crest Publishers

Snoop Dogg

FRONTIS Rapper, producer, businessman, and avid gamer Snoop Dogg hosts Spike
TV's 2004 Video Game Awards.

PRODUCED BY 21ST CENTURY PUBLISHING AND COMMUNICATIONS, INC.

MASON CREST PUBLISHERS INC.
370 Reed Road
Broomall, Pennsylvania 19008
(866)MCP-BOOK (toll free)
www.masoncrest.com

Printed in the U.S.A.

First Printing

9 8 7 6 5 4 3 2 1

Library of Congress Cataloging-in-Publication Data

Carlson-Berne, Emma.
    Snoop Dogg / Emma Carlson-Berne.
       p. cm. — (Hip-hop)
    Includes bibliographical references (p.   ) and index.
Hardback edition: ISBN-13: 978-1-4222-0129-9
Hardback edition: ISBN-10: 1-4222-0129-5
Paperback edition: ISBN-13: 978-1-4222-0279-1
1. Snoop Dogg, 1972–   2. Rap musicians—UnitedStates—Biography—Juvenile
literature. I. Title. II. Series.
ML3930.S68B47 2007
782.421649092—dc22
[B]   2006011812

Contents

Hip-Hop Timeline

1974 Hip-hop pioneer Afrika Bambaataa organizes the Universal Zulu Nation.

1988 *Yo! MTV Raps* premieres on MTV.

1970s Hip-hop as a cultural movement begins in the Bronx, New York City.

1985 *Krush Groove*, a hip-hop film about Def Jam Recordings, is released featuring Run-D.M.C., Kurtis Blow, LL Cool J, and the Beastie Boys.

1970s DJ Kool Herc pioneers the use of breaks, isolations, and repeats using two turntables.

1979 The Sugarhill Gang's song "Rapper's Delight" is the first hip-hop single to go gold.

1986 Run-D.M.C. are the first rappers to appear on the cover of *Rolling Stone* magazine.

1970   **1980**   **1988**

1976 Grandmaster Flash & the Furious Five pioneer hip-hop MCing and freestyle battles.

1986 Beastie Boys' album *Licensed to Ill* is released and becomes the best-selling rap album of the 1980s.

1970s Break dancing emerges at parties and in public places in New York City.

1982 Afrika Bambaataa embarks on the first European hip-hop tour.

1988 Hip-hop music annual record sales reaches $100 million.

1970s Graffiti artist Vic pioneers tagging on subway trains in New York City.

1984 *Graffiti Rock*, the first hip-hop television program, premieres.

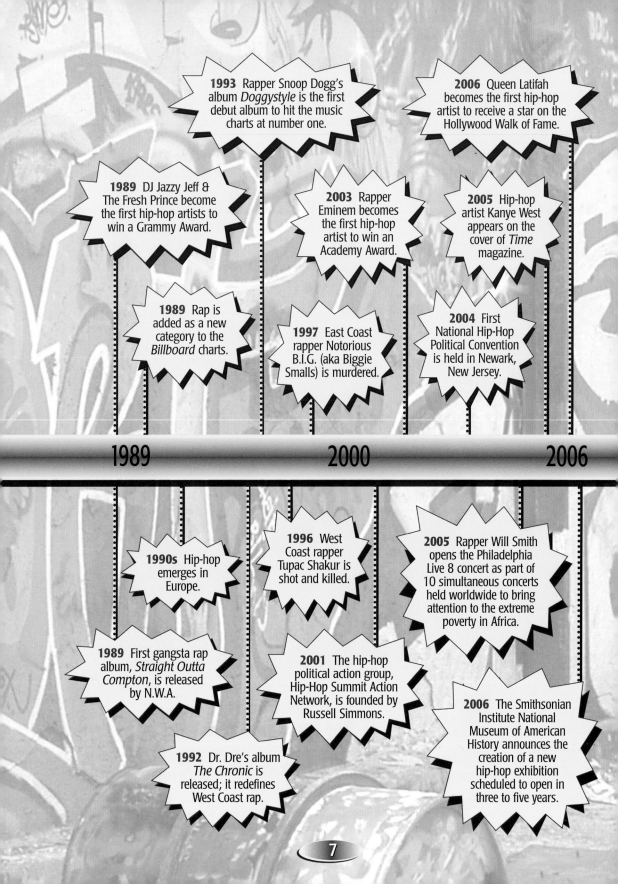

1993 Rapper Snoop Dogg's album *Doggystyle* is the first debut album to hit the music charts at number one.

2006 Queen Latifah becomes the first hip-hop artist to receive a star on the Hollywood Walk of Fame.

1989 DJ Jazzy Jeff & The Fresh Prince become the first hip-hop artists to win a Grammy Award.

2003 Rapper Eminem becomes the first hip-hop artist to win an Academy Award.

2005 Hip-hop artist Kanye West appears on the cover of *Time* magazine.

1989 Rap is added as a new category to the *Billboard* charts.

1997 East Coast rapper Notorious B.I.G. (aka Biggie Smalls) is murdered.

2004 First National Hip-Hop Political Convention is held in Newark, New Jersey.

1989   **2000**   **2006**

1990s Hip-hop emerges in Europe.

1996 West Coast rapper Tupac Shakur is shot and killed.

2005 Rapper Will Smith opens the Philadelphia Live 8 concert as part of 10 simultaneous concerts held worldwide to bring attention to the extreme poverty in Africa.

1989 First gangsta rap album, *Straight Outta Compton*, is released by N.W.A.

2001 The hip-hop political action group, Hip-Hop Summit Action Network, is founded by Russell Simmons.

2006 The Smithsonian Institute National Museum of American History announces the creation of a new hip-hop exhibition scheduled to open in three to five years.

1992 Dr. Dre's album *The Chronic* is released; it redefines West Coast rap.

Snoop Dogg performs at the Live 8 concert in Hyde Park, London. The concert was intended to show leaders of the world's most developed nations that citizens care about poverty in Africa and want their countries to help.

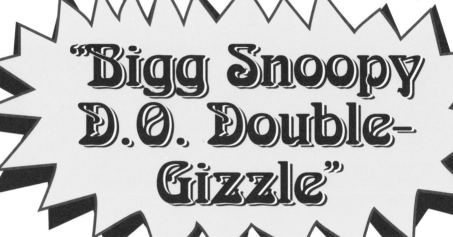

1

"Bigg Snoopy D.O. Double-Gizzle"

Rapper Snoop Dogg's powerful lyrics riveted the enormous crowd at the Live 8 concert in London on July 2, 2005. In a message heard by nearly 10 million people, Snoop proclaimed that the world must erase poverty in Africa. He was, after all, in his own words, "the President of the United Ghettos of the World, Bigg Snoopy D.O. Double-Gizzle!"

The Live 8 concert would be a high point in any performer's career, but success is nothing new for the Doggfather. Throughout the years, Snoop has been praised by critics and fans for his silky, hypnotic voice and **evocative**, **provocative** lyrics that paint images of life on the streets. Getting his start under the influential rapper and music producer Dr. Dre, Snoop was part of the massive popularization of gangsta rap when he appeared on Dre's highly influential album *The Chronic*. His solo album *Doggystyle* is the only debut album in history to hit the *Billboard* charts at number one. Since that auspicious beginning, seven of Snoop's ten records have gone **platinum** with two going double platinum. *Doggystyle* eventually went platinum four times and stayed at number one for three weeks on the U.S. charts.

Rocking the World

Snoop's influence on people is a big part of the reason he was asked to perform during the Live 8 concert. This massive worldwide event consisted of one giant concert held *simultaneously* in nine cities around the world: London, Paris, Berlin, Rome, Philadelphia, Tokyo, Moscow, Johannesburg, and Barrie, Canada. The concert sought to bring the world's attention to the problem of poverty in Africa. It was held right before the 2005 G8 summit, an annual meeting in which eight of the leaders of the world's major industrialized countries gather to discuss global problems. The organizers and performers of the Live 8 concert wanted to influence the G8 members to help Africa's countries out of their extreme poverty.

The concert was a huge success. Some of the biggest names in music were there: Elton John, Madonna, U2, and, of course, the Dogg. An estimated 3 *billion* people listened or watched around the world as Madonna danced with a young African famine survivor, Sting played a piano solo, and Snoop Dogg showed off his moves. Jack Foley of the music Web site IndieLondon wrote in a review:

> **"[Snoop] lived up to his reputation to deliver a genuinely thrilling set that had everyone watching in awe . . . the stage was alive with the booty-shaking rhythms of hip-hop's favourite son, effortlessly tapping into the spirit of the Live 8 occasion and making everyone sing along."**

Snoop in particular felt a passion for the Live 8 message because of his own background. While on stage, he said:

> **"America is one place where you can go from nothing to something. . . . I come from the hood in Long Beach, and now, I'm a boss of the entertainment industry—and it feels real good to be working**

During the Live 8 show, Snoop Dogg told the audience that he wanted everyone in Africa to have the same kind of opportunity that he had to succeed. Organizers of the concerts were asking that Africa's poor countries be forgiven their debts.

with Live 8 to share the same opportunity for progress with my people in Africa . . . so don't forget to make the choice to change our world."

While is it impossible to say what impact the Live 8 concert had on the G8 summit, the industrialized nations did agree to provide more assistance to Africa. Eighteen of the most heavily indebted poor countries were forgiven debts amounting to $40 billion, and the G8 also agreed to double aid to poor countries by the year 2010. These agreements met some of the demands of the Live 8 organizers, though certainly not all. The G8 made no progress on environmental and trade issues, leaving those concerns for another time.

Snoop Dogg poses with an Iraq war veteran who was helped by the Fisher House Foundation, July 2005. Snoop performed at the Salute to the Troops charity event in Honolulu, Hawaii, which raised money for Fisher House.

Support Our Troops

Snoop's desire to help people also spurred him to perform that same month at a charity concert for 8,000 members of the military and their families in Honolulu, Hawaii. The July 24 event was sponsored by Bodog, an online gambling Web site. The money from the concert went to help the Fisher House Foundation, a charity that provides families places to stay when they are visiting an injured soldier.

Clad in a red, white, and blue "Support Our Troops" jersey, with his hair in his trademark braids, Snoop led the audience in call-and-response chants and dances. The fans loved it. Maria Starr of Bodog wrote in a review posted on their website that, "based on fan reaction alone it was crystal clear that Snoop's show delivered big time. The show kicked." Snoop admitted that he had a great time himself. "It's a beautiful feeling to be appreciated and come out and give the troops something to smile about and something to dance to. . . . I'm down to do it again whenever, however, forever, all the time," he told *Vibe* magazine's Alyssa Rashbaum in an interview.

Over the last decade, Snoop has become one of America's most popular rap artists. His recipe for success—combining razor-sharp lyrics with provocative subject matter, a dash of playfulness, and a pinch of anger—has proven irresistible. The lean physique and squinty eyes are instantly recognizable to millions of people. But although his face is famous today, at one time he was just a poor skinny kid with a lot of dreams and a lot of talent.

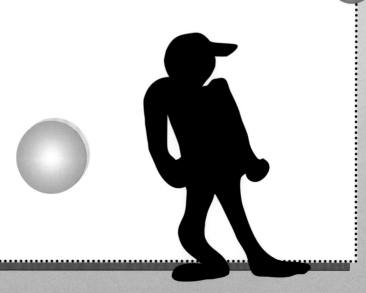

Snoop Dogg acquired his nickname, Snoopy, when he was very little. No one knows quite where the name came from, but when he started rapping as a teenager, it was only natural that it would become part of his stage name.

2

Growing Up in the LBC

Snoop was born Calvin Cordozar Broadus on October 20, 1971, at the Los Altos hospital in Long Beach, California. No one really knows where he got his famous nickname. One story goes that his mother said he looked like Snoopy from the Peanuts comic. Another says he got the name from his stepfather. Somehow, though, the name Snoopy stuck.

Calvin's mother, Beverly Broadus Green, had grown up in the small rural town of McComb, Mississippi. The family was very poor, and Beverly's father was an abusive alcoholic. Beverly remembers a happy childhood, but her mother grew tired of her husband's drinking. In 1963 she took a vacation to Long Beach. Two weeks later she sent word to her brother to pack up the children, including the teenage Beverly, and move the entire family to California.

As a young woman, Beverly had a complicated set of relationships with various men. She first met the boy who would be Calvin's biological father, Vernell Varnado, when they both were in high school. They fell in love and agreed to stay faithful to each other even after Vernell went into the army.

Soon, however, Beverly started dating a sailor named Harold Carter. She became pregnant by him with Snoop's older brother Jerry. The relationship fizzled; and while still pregnant and in high school, Beverly met another sailor, this one named Al Cordozar Broadus. They married in 1970 soon after Beverly's graduation.

Life did not settle down for Beverly, though. She was still in touch with Vernell, and he came for a visit when he was discharged from the army. During that visit Beverly became pregnant with Vernell's child, Calvin, though she was still married to Al Broadus. Fearing Al's reaction when he learned she had cheated on him, she told him the baby was his. Both Calvin and Al believed that Al was the real father up until his death of a heart attack in 1984. Beverly had her third and final baby, Bing, in 1979 with another boyfriend, Bing Worthington. That relationship also did not last. For the rest of Calvin's childhood, his mother cycled through boyfriend after boyfriend. None lasted, and many were abusive to Beverly, Calvin, and his brothers.

Life in Long Beach

The Broadus family suffered hard times while Snoop was growing up. Their neighborhood, the eastern section of Long Beach, was run-down and riddled with crime. Drug deals took place openly on the streets in front of the Broadus home. Shootings occurred on a regular basis, most of them related to drugs. The family lived in poverty, and Beverly struggled with alcohol and drug addiction in addition to her unstable relationships. Calvin tried to help out his mother and brothers by selling candy, delivering newspapers, and bagging groceries. Despite these hardships, he remembers his childhood as a happy one. He says in his autobiography, *Tha Doggfather*:

> **"Most of the memories I have growing up aren't a whole lot different from the ones you've got. Kids are kids and they mostly are wanting and needing and hoping for the same kind of things no matter what side of the tracks they call home."**

Snoop's Early Influences

Throughout his entire childhood, Calvin was extremely close to his mom. She was the constant in his life. Beverly gave him unconditional love and support. He writes in *Tha Doggfather*:

> **"The earliest memories I have are of my mama's loving me, holding me close, kissing my face and stroking my head and making me feel safe and secure and special in a way that only your mama can. Because of her, and her alone, there was never a time that I went without, never a minute when I didn't believe that I could do anything I put my heart and mind to, never a doubt that I had what it took to make something of myself."**

It was Beverly who taught Snoop to be an independent person and have the self-confidence to try new things, even when it seemed impossible. "[She gave me] the feeling that I was worth something," Snoop wrote. "When you're little and weak . . . you got to have a champion, someone to look out for you. . . . What my mama told me, every day of my life, was that she had faith in me, all the way."

Beverly worked extremely hard to support her sons. At one point she had two jobs: cleaning in a nursing home and serving food in a school cafeteria. Still, she found time to take care of her family as well. Beverly would often make little Calvin's favorite dishes: chicken wings and macaroni and cheese.

Beverly was deeply religious and made time to instill spirituality in her sons as well. The whole family attended Trinity Baptist Church every Sunday and Tuesday, where Calvin sang in the choir. Snoop recalls his mother's faith as being much more than just following church rules:

> **"She had a one-on-one connection to God, a way of talking with Him like He was in the same room or on the phone line, a free and easy flow, passing the time with her closest friend. She *knew* God heard her prayers, knew it like she knew her own face in the mirror, and she passed that confidence along to us, making sure we understood that, whatever we might be lacking in a father, God would make up for and then some."**

Beverly's faith gave her family strength and comfort. "[N]one of us kids ever felt underprivileged, disadvantaged, or inferior to anyone we might pass on the street, white or black. Mama loved us. God loved us. Nothing else mattered," Snoop wrote in *Tha Doggfather*.

Like spirituality, love of music ran in little Calvin's blood. Though he didn't know him growing up, his biological father, Vernell, sang in a gospel trio during his own young adulthood. Vernell continued his musical pursuits on and off as an adult, sometimes collaborating with

Rapper Snoop Doggy Dogg is pictured here with his mother Beverly Broadus. She is carrying Snoop's young son, Corde. Snoop credits his mother for instilling in him the confidence to succeed in the hip-hop world.

his brothers and eventually putting out a record or two. Calvin would occasionally hear reports of his father's progress. Beverly encouraged her son to play the piano and would frequently sing along as he played. Snoop remembers listening to his mother's 1970s blues and **funk** records over and over. Artists like Johnnie Taylor, the Dramatics, and Curtis Mayfield helped shape his early tastes. Snoop says that if it weren't for his mother's influence, he may never have grown up to be a professional musician himself.

Being surrounded by music, it seemed natural for Calvin to start making up music of his own. He composed his first rap, "Super Rhymes," while in the sixth grade at Lafayette Elementary School in Long Beach. By the time he was 15, Snoop was a well-known figure in the neighborhood. He was rapping regularly and frequently won the freestyle MC competitions that took place in the schoolyard and on the street. He and friend Warren G would practice rapping to one another constantly.

Snoop and Warren met when they were just six and seven years old and soon became close friends. They supported each other's interest in rap at a time when no one else they knew really cared about it. They both got a job selling candy door-to-door in upper-middle class suburbs. "G and I would try out raps on each other during those long afternoons walking around rich white streets, flowing on anything and everything we could think of," Snoop wrote in his autobiography. By the time Warren G and Snoop were older teenagers, they were rapping together all the time and had formed a group called 213 with a third friend, Nate Dogg.

> **We just liked the sound of our own voices. We liked cracking each other up with stories about the little everyday things that happened in our lives, putting ourselves into the plots of movies and TV shows, or just dreaming out loud about all the fine scrilla we'd put together with what we'd earned at the end of the day. . . . That was some of the best rapping I ever did, even to this day.**

Unlike other music styles, rap was considered more democratic and easier for poor kids to pick up. "If you think you got what it takes, there's nothing stopping you from giving it a shot. You don't need a

Rappers Warren G (left), Snoop Doggy Dogg (center), and Nate Dogg (right) perform during the Rock the Vote Bus Tour. During the early 1990s the three rappers performed as 213, a group named after the area code for their homes in Long Beach, California.

music degree, or ten years of saxophone lessons or a forty-eight-track studio to bust a move," Snoop wrote in *Tha Doggfather*.

During his teens, Snoop fell in with a gang called the Crips. The Crips were famous for their deadly feud with another gang, the Bloods. Snoop had mixed feelings about being a Crip, but the gang provided a community for its members, a sense of belonging that many young African-American men growing up in poverty did not feel very often.

Later in his life, Snoop told *Rolling Stone* interviewer Erik Hedegaard that the power and **camaraderie** of the gang were exciting:

> **"**You know, . . . the money, the cars, the jewelry, the respect; people knowing my . . . name; knowing who I was, what I stood for . . . that's a hell of a thing the gang gives you.**"**

Prison Life

Snoop couldn't escape the consequences of the gang lifestyle, though. In 1990 he was caught selling **crack cocaine** to an undercover police officer and was sentenced to a year in Wayside Jail in Anaheim, California. He had just graduated from high school. For the next year, Snoop composed raps and performed them for his fellow prison inmates, who felt that he was too talented to be wasting his life away behind bars. Snoop made up his mind to get serious about rap once he got out. He regretted the behavior that landed him in jail, saying in later interviews that selling drugs was wrong and dangerous. He discouraged children from following his example.

Part of what kept Snoop going while he was in jail was the steady support of his best friend, Warren G. Warren kept in touch with Snoop and encouraged him not to stop rapping. Aside from support, Warren also gave Snoop something almost as important as his friendship; he got Snoop his first big break.

This publicity photo of Snoop Doggy Dogg was issued by Death Row Records during the early 1990s. Snoop was recruited to join Death Row after coming to the attention of the label's cofounder, Dr. Dre, the half-brother of Snoop's friend Warren G.

3

From Ghetto to Superstar

In 1991, less than one year after Snoop got out of prison, his group 213 recorded a demo tape and sold 500 copies out of the trunk of a car. They knew their tape was popular among their friends and acquaintances in Long Beach. What they didn't know was that the entire rap world was ready for their new sound.

Hip-hop had been in existence since the early 1970s, but it was constantly evolving. During the mid-1980s, a new sound in rap was starting to emerge from the gritty, poverty-stricken streets of Los Angeles, created by young people who had something to say about the gangs, drugs, and crime they saw around them. This new sound was called gangsta rap. It differed from previous forms of hip-hop in its violent lyrics that described, and sometimes celebrated, life on the streets. Drug use was glorified. Violence against women was treated as normal and acceptable. Those who were opposed to gangsta rap felt that there was nothing of value in what the music had to say. They believed that it could only hurt the children that listened to it.

In the musicians' defense, some argued that gangsta rappers spoke about a life they had actually lived as members of street gangs, making their music a kind of documentary that did not glorify violence so much as it told the truth. Others suggested that in the songs, the rappers were merely playing a role, much as an actor in a play would. This stance proposed that the music was no more instructional for children than an action film. Proponents also pointed out that violence on the streets really exists and should not be hidden or covered up.

The Father of Gangsta Rap

In the midst of this new sound and its accompanying controversy stood Warren G's half-brother, a man named Dr. Dre. Dre, whose real name is Andre Young, is credited with both the founding of gangsta rap and the introduction of the genre to the larger musical world. His group N.W.A (Niggaz With Attitude), released the first mainstream album of gangsta rap, *Straight Outta Compton*, in 1989. Its success opened the door wide for other gangsta rappers.

Dre is a talented musician in his own right, but he has made his name mainly by discovering young, gifted rappers and then collaborating with them to release their albums. In 1991 he and rap **impresario** Suge Knight started a record label called Death Row Records. It became one of the most well-known and respected rap labels in the industry.

Dr. Dre had a good ear for hot new music, and when his half-brother Warren G came to him one day in 1991 and asked him to listen to a demo tape he had recorded with his group, Dre agreed. Warren's group included a young rapper no one had heard of named Snoop Doggy Dogg. When Dre heard his smooth drawl on the scratchy, homemade tape, he knew he had found his next star.

Collaboration

Dr. Dre invited Snoop to make an appearance on an album he was currently producing, the soundtrack to the film *Deep Cover*. Snoop appeared with Dre on the title track. The soundtrack as a whole was underwhelming to rap fans and critics, but the smooth young voice in the title song did not go unnoticed. "Where other rappers bark threats, [Snoop] purrs warnings with a feline dispassion," says Rob Tannenbaum of *Blender* magazine. Dr. Dre's lyrics combined with Snoop's delivery worked to create something powerful and disturbing.

Dr. Dre began his career as a rapper and producer with the influential group N.W.A, whose groundbreaking 1989 album *Straight Outta Compton* helped define the genre known as "gangsta rap." Dissatisfied with his record label, Dre formed Death Row with Marion "Suge" Knight.

After the reviews of *Deep Cover* started coming in, Dr. Dre realized that he had found an unparalleled musical performer in Snoop Doggy Dogg. In 1992 Dre asked Snoop to appear on his first album with Death Row Records. As Snoop and Dre laid down tracks in recording studios all across L.A. that year, something fresh started to emerge from their sessions. They found themselves creating tunes with a hypnotic bass line, synthesizers, and female vocals in the background. This combination of funk music and gangsta rap was compelling and intensely danceable. After *The Chronic*'s release, music critics started calling it G-funk—gangsta-funk.

In *The Chronic* Snoop and Dre took their flowing, lazy sound and combined it with some of the most violent and profane lyrics rap fans had ever heard. They poured out anthems of murder, sex, and drugs. "We took that gang-bang violence in us and projected that violence into music instead," Snoop explained in *Blender* magazine years after the album's release.

The Sky Is the Limit

The Chronic was a huge commercial success. It went platinum three times, eventually peaking at number three on the music charts. But more important than just sales was the fact that for the first time people everywhere started listening to gangsta rap. Kids in the suburbs were dancing to cleaned-up versions of the album's hit single, "Nuttin' But A 'G' Thang" at school dances. College students were spinning the tunes at house parties.

Critics and fans alike agreed that *The Chronic*'s funky sound and brash lyrics would have faded into obscurity were it not for Snoop's incredibly laid-back demeanor contrasting with the extreme violence of the lyrics. The combination was irresistible. Steve Huey, a critic who reviewed *The Chronic* for AllMusic, an online music source, wrote, "Snoop livens up every track he touches . . . there [is] nothing in rap quite like Snoop's singsong, lazy drawl. . . . He sounds utterly unaffected by anything, no matter how extreme, which sets the tone for the album's **misogyny**, **homophobia**, and violence." But the success also came with controversy. Women's groups, African-American political groups, and community leaders objected strongly to the album's lyrics. In 1993 a coalition of women's groups protested when a *Chronic* tour date was scheduled for New York City. The coalition told the *New York Daily News* that Dr. Dre and his rappers were degrading African-American

SPECIAL FIRST ANNIVERSARY ISSUE

BLAZE

EXCLUSIVE! DISSECTING THE '90s WITH
DR. DRE & SNOOP

TUPAC BIGGIE LAURYN BUSTA PUFFY SUGE PRIMO L.L. KRRL KANI WU-TANG OUTKAS

FOXY MA... ...CE CUBE HYPE WILLIAMS FUNK FLEX DJ C... ...VIBE HAMMER

This issue of *Blaze* magazine from 1999, marking its first anniversary, features Dr. Dre and Snoop Dogg. In the magazine's lead article, Dre and Snoop Dogg are credited with shaping the sound of hip-hop in the 1990s.

Rapper Snoop Doggy Dogg poses after the 1994 MTV Video Music Awards. He won an award for Best Rap Video for "Doggy Dogg World" from the album *Doggystyle*. The album was Snoop's first to debut at number one on the charts.

women by using words such as "bitch," "ho," and "the n-word." They eventually succeeded in keeping Dre from performing at Madison Square Garden.

Snoop doesn't deny what these critics have said—he admits that a lot of his lyrics do not depict women in a healthy way. But the fact that the songs have a certain attitude does not mean that Snoop, himself, has that same attitude. In his book he carefully explained that in his personal life, he treats women with respect.

Dogg in the House

After the success of *The Chronic*, Dr. Dre and Snoop Doggy Dogg went to work putting out Snoop's debut solo album for Death Row Records. In September 1993 *Doggystyle* was released, containing 14 tracks featuring Snoop's signature sound. *Doggystyle* became the first debut album in history to hit the music charts at number one. It went on to sell over 5 million copies and establish Snoop's reputation as a top rapper in his own right.

The money and attention poured in. Critics for *Rolling Stone*, *Billboard*, and *Vibe* magazines discussed his hot new sound in the pages of their publications, and radio DJs fielded calls from listeners requesting Snoop's songs dozens of times a day. He was on the cover of three major music magazines.

But Snoop's success also brought new complications to his life. He struggled to protect his image but did not always make good choices. In one early photo shoot, for instance, he posed with a gun—a decision he later said he regretted. He spent money lavishly on houses, cars, and long fur coats. As his fame increased, Snoop also became increasingly worried about his personal safety. His ties to the Crips were well known. In *Tha Doggfather* Snoop wrote, "what had me worried was the fact that, because of my high profile, I was a sitting duck for the ongoing turf war between the Crips and the Bloods."

During the mid-1990s, Snoop Dogg's life was plagued by violence. In 1993 he was involved in a deadly shooting in Los Angeles and placed on trial for murder. In 1996, the year his trial ended, Snoop's friend Tupac Shakur was shot and killed.

4

Hard Times

Despite his worries, Snoop Doggy Dogg was a happy man in the summer of 1993. *Doggystyle* was almost completed. And he was about to become a father. Shante Taylor and Snoop had been together since they were both in high school, and she was pregnant with their first baby, a boy named Corde.

Shante and Snoop had grown up in the same neighborhood. They had known one another since Snoop was a poor kid like all the other kids in the neighborhood. Shante stuck by Snoop when he was in jail. And she was still with him when he was writing rhymes for Dr. Dre. With Shante, Snoop never had to worry that she was only with him for his money and fame; she had loved him long before he had anything but dreams. In his auto-biography Snoop wrote that he and Shante have always had a special bond.

"Before I ever even knew I loved her, or ever thought about asking her to be my wife, Shante was my friend, my number one homegirl, and the one person I trusted with my deepest and darkest secrets."

Changed in an Instant

Snoop had a lot going for him that summer. But on August 24, 1993, a hot sunny day, he almost lost everything. Much of what happened that day has been disputed, but this much is clear: Snoop was closely involved in the fatal shooting of a rival gang member named Philip Woldemariam. He was arrested, booked as an **accomplice**, and sent to jail to wait for his hearing. All of a sudden his bright future appeared uncertain.

In court the facts became clearer. A group of gang members that included Woldemariam had been driving around in a suburb of Los Angeles one afternoon when they thought they saw someone in another group standing outside an apartment building flash a rival gang sign. Woldemariam and his friends did not know that this was Snoop Dogg's crew, because Snoop and his bodyguard had gone upstairs to an apartment. Woldemariam flashed his gang sign back and traded insults. His group drove off to a nearby park. Soon Snoop appeared driving a Jeep with Malik Lee, his bodyguard, in the seat next to him. The two groups argued. Woldemariam approached the car, and Lee shot him, claiming that the other man had been reaching for a gun.

Snoop was arrested for his part in the crime immediately after appearing as a presenter at the MTV Video Music Awards. The murder trial lasted for four months, from November 1995 until February 1996. Snoop was eventually **acquitted**, but the experience left deep scars. He told Dave Wielenga of *Rolling Stone* magazine:

> **"What I've been through has changed me for the better. . . . If I'm gonna come back, I wanna come back right. . . . I'm gonna step up and handle my position, as far as trying to be the role model I tried to deny at the beginning of my career. I was a follower. Now I look at myself as a leader."**

Losing A Friend

Snoop had even more difficulties ahead of him. Although he was intimately familiar with homicides, he had never experienced the loss of someone truly close to him. That changed with the September 1996 murder of his good friend, rapper and fellow Death Row Records star Tupac Shakur.

Snoop Dogg bows his head in relief after hearing the not-guilty verdict at his murder trial. It was revealed in court that the victim, Philip Woldemariam, had been reaching for his own weapon, and jurors decided the shooting was in self-defense.

Los Angeles-based Death Row had gained notoriety as a key player in a rivalry between rappers on the west and east coasts. Tupac, in particular, developed a special rivalry with the Notorious B.I.G., a rapper from New York who was on the Bad Boy Entertainment label. Tupac believed the Notorious B.I.G. had set him up to be murdered in a New York recording studio in 1994.

In Las Vegas on September 7, 1996, a white Cadillac pulled up beside a BMW carrying Tupac and Suge Knight. A man in the back of the Cadillac stuck a gun out the window and fired multiple times into Knight's car. Tupac was hit three times. Although he was eventually taken to a hospital, Tupac fell into a coma. Six days later he died.

Tupac's death hit the entire rap world hard. The 25-year-old had been one of the most popular, vital, and controversial rappers on the scene. For fans and critics alike, he embodied much of the good and

Snoop Dogg (center) poses with fellow Death Row star Tupac Shakur (left) and label cofounder Marion "Suge" Knight (right). Death Row Records, based in Los Angeles, California, had great success promoting the West Coast "gangsta rap" sound.

bad of gangsta rap. Tupac was smart and charismatic, and his music drew listeners in. But he also thrived on controversy. His lyrics were as violent and profane as any gangsta rap had ever seen. He rapped about killing cops, taking drugs, and fighting on the streets. Tupac was also known for living the thug life he rapped about. He had already been shot five times in a previous incident, and he had been indicted on sexual assault charges.

Some people believed that Tupac had made the bed he died in by glorifying violence in his lyrics. Many others in the press held Tupac's death up as an example of the dangers of the gangsta lifestyle and its music. Across the country, a popular **backlash** against gangsta rap had begun.

At home in California, Snoop mourned the loss of his friend. It was a frightening time. No one knew who had killed Tupac, but Snoop and the other Death Row rappers feared it was a hit by the Notorious B.I.G. and his east coast crew. In the midst of trying to accept the loss of his friend, Snoop worried he might be next. It made the danger and

Rapper Notorious B.I.G. from Brooklyn poses at the 1995 *Billboard* Music Awards. Notorious B.I.G. (also called Biggie Smalls) was signed to Bad Boy Entertainment, the east coast rival of Death Row. A feud between Tupac and Biggie may have contributed to their deaths.

tragedy of their world very clear. "We've got to stop killing each other," he wrote in *Tha Doggfather*. "We've got to turn our rage and our righteous anger on the target where it belongs—the system that keeps us oppressed and down and addicted to crack and attacking in the dead of night like wild animals tearing at each other's throats."

Hitting Bottom

The hard times weren't over yet. Soon after Tupac's death, Snoop's manager, Sharitha Knight (Suge's wife), sued him, claiming that he owed her millions of dollars in management fees. To make matters worse, Snoop discovered that Death Row had not been paying him **royalties** from his albums and had been taking his publishing rights, all the while showering him with jewelry and cars and paying his legal fees from his murder trial so that he might not notice. These were not the terms of his contract. Snoop was still relatively new to the business and did not keep very good track of his earnings, so he didn't realize he wasn't being paid the proper amount. To compound these problems, Snoop's second album, *Tha Doggfather*, released in November 1996, was not selling as well as expected due to the backlash against gangsta rap.

This was one of the lowest points in Snoop's career. He was broke. His record label had cheated him. He was being sued. Dr. Dre had left Death Row Records and started a new label. He had no manager. He feared for his life and spent much of his time hiding. And his album wasn't selling. But Snoop was not going to give up.

Love and Marriage

Ever since his involvement in the shooting of Philip Woldemariam, Snoop had spent a lot of time thinking about the decisions he had made over the years. He thought about his long relationship with Shante, who had borne him two children—his sons, Corde and Cordell. And he decided that he needed to get his priorities in order and focus on the family that loved him. In 1997 he and Shante got married.

Shante and Snoop proved that they had what it takes to stay together through tough times, even before their marriage. When you're with a woman you love, Snoop wrote in his autobiography, "sooner or later you'll be waking up to the cold, hard facts that love at first sight doesn't last forever and what it takes to get through with someone is hanging in, one day at a time, for better or worse, till death do you part."

Snoop and Shante's relationship has not been easy. They have fought a lot, and living as the wife of a rap star puts extra pressure on Shante. She has to deal with media attention wherever she goes, even when she wants privacy. Her husband's actions are being constantly scrutinized in the public eye, and this has occasionally strained their marriage. Shante has never wavered in her support for Snoop though, especially during the hardest times in his life.

Snoop Dogg and his wife, Shante, have been together since they were young adults living in Long Beach. According to Snoop, the ghetto doesn't teach people what real love is like. He and Shante have been figuring it out the hard way.

Pondering the Past

Around the time of his wedding, Snoop was still spending a lot of time thinking. He was very happy with Shante, but he still felt haunted by Tupac's death. Losing his friend had been like a bucket of ice water poured on his head. He wrote in his autobiography:

After Tupac's death, Snoop Dogg spent a lot of time pondering life and what he wanted to really do with himself. The loss of his friend served as a reminder that he needed to commit himself to the things he really wanted.

"Sometimes, if you're lucky, someone comes into your life who'll take up a place in your heart no one else can fill, someone who's tighter than a twin, more with you than your own shadow, who gets deeper under your skin than your own blood and bones."

He'd found such a friend and lost him. It made Snoop think critically about the mind-set and atmosphere in the rap world. He began to talk more about being a role model for black youth. He started questioning some of gangsta rap's most violent lyrics and attitudes. He wrote in his autobiography, "It wasn't enough just to tell it like it is anymore. It was time to tell it like it could be."

Tupac was gone, but his influence had remained. Snoop thought about the best part of his friend—his commitment to his music—and took that to heart. He told Sarah Rodman in the *Boston Herald* in 1997:

"[Tupac's] ethics rubbed off on me. . . . I've just been a workaholic, and I got that from him because he used to always just work, work, work. There's no such thing as too much, that's what he taught me."

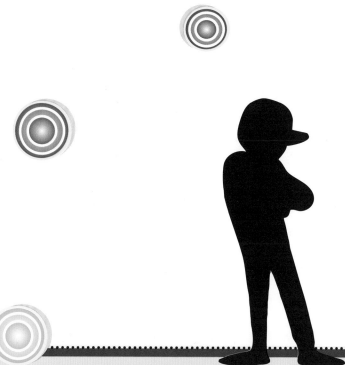

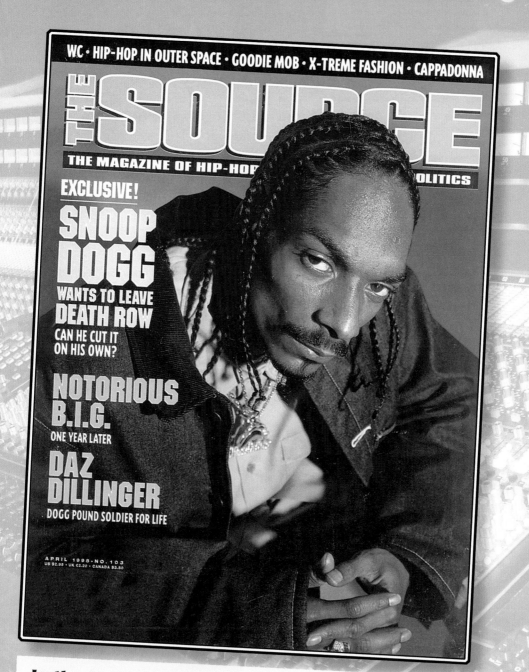

In the April 1998 issue of *The Source* magazine, Snoop Dogg discussed his desire to leave Death Row Records. Snoop eventually did break with the label, joining Master P's record label No Limit. The change brought him renewed creativity.

5

Tha Dogg Rises Again

Snoop wanted to keep rapping, but his relationship with Death Row Records was in shambles. So in 1998 he announced he was splitting with the record label that had given him his start. He started looking around for a new label and soon found a home at No Limit Records.

The success of No Limit Records was mostly due to the hard work and charisma of the CEO, Master P. Under his direction, No Limit became a major production company in only three years. In 1998 Master P made enough money to earn a place on *Forbes* magazine's list of highest-earning American entertainers.

When he joined No Limit, Snoop's career needed a jumpstart. He had been mired in personal problems and needed a source of inspiration. A new environment and new producer gave him the boost he was looking for. In short order Snoop released four albums under the No Limit label: *Da Game Is To Be Sold, Not To Be Told* in 1998, *Topp Dogg* in 1999, and *Dead Man Walkin'* and *Tha Last Meal* in 2000. The albums sold moderately well.

Some critics attributed the drop in sales to the fact that Master P liked the songs coming out of his label to have a consistent sound. When Snoop's first album with No Limit came out, it lacked his previous flair. Neil Strauss, a music journalist from *Rolling Stone*, said in 1998 that Snoop's trademark lines "have been put through the No Limit assembly line, turned into marketing techniques designed to sell an album and make its songs ring familiar."

By working with No Limit, Snoop's life changed as much as his music. In 1998 he, Master P, and other rappers caused a stir when they moved together to an upscale, gated community outside of Baton Rouge, Louisiana, that had not had a black resident since 1993. The move was made for the simplest of reasons. Master P wanted his children to grow up in a safe suburban environment. At first the community was wary of the rappers; the country club even refused them admission. But Snoop and the others proved themselves pillars of the community, giving generously to local charities and schools.

From Gangsta to Pimp

Snoop's move to the gated community also marked the start of a major shift in his image. He was married, and his children were growing up. Tupac's death and the fighting among rappers had put off many rap fans, so sales dropped. But Snoop wasn't ready to retire just yet; he decided that he needed an image makeover.

Snoop gathered a group of savvy businesspeople to advise him. They told him that in order to keep his record sales up, he needed to reach out to a broader range of people. He needed to make music that people who weren't strictly gangsta rap fans would listen to, and they suggested that he portray himself differently.

So Snoop began his shift from, as he called it, "gangsta" to "pimp." Strictly speaking, a "pimp" is someone who finds customers for a prostitute. But Snoop says that for him, being a pimp means "feeling good, dressing good, and no one's stepping on your alligator shoes." In other words, Snoop believed that to be a "pimp" meant acting the part of a rich man, rather than a kid from the streets.

Snoop made the leap easily. His album *Paid tha Cost To Be da Bo$$*, released in November 2002, incorporated more of his early influences, like 1970s funk from Bobby Womack and the O'Jays. Snoop also started dressing differently. He discarded his super-baggy blue jeans and do-rags and began wearing custom-tailored silk suits, alligator shoes, and long mink coats. He had a Cadillac Coupe de Ville custom made with several TV screens and mink-lined seats. He even began drinking from a personalized, rhinestone-covered goblet at all of his public appearances.

This publicity photo was taken around the time that *Paid tha Cost To Be da Bo$$* was released in 2002. In addition to a new musical direction, Snoop began shedding his gangsta image, instead adopting what he called the "pimp" look.

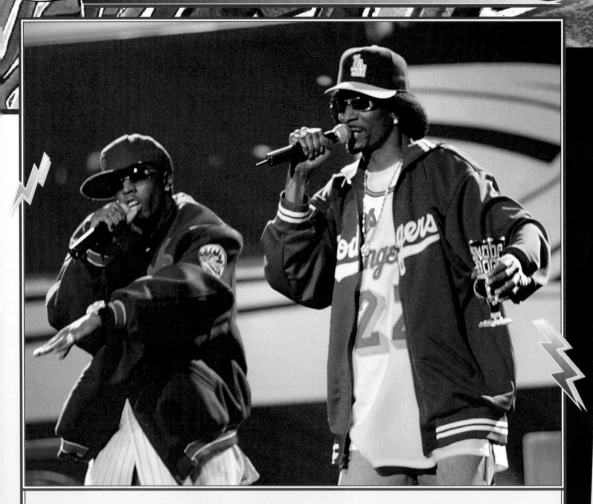

Rappers Sean Combs and Snoop Dogg perform at the 29th annual American Music Awards in Los Angeles, January 2002. Snoop is holding the rhinestone-encrusted goblet that he started using at public appearances as part of his new image.

Planet Snoop

Snoop's image makeover was a huge success, and his sales began to go up. As his image became more polished and his music less hardcore and violent, Snoop became more acceptable to many more people—not just teenagers but adults of different races and backgrounds. Soon big companies began to see him as a potential spokesman, and they approached him with lucrative contracts. Snoop embraced these new opportunities and began doing commercials for cell phones, juice drinks, and video games. Snoop Dogg was becoming a brand all his own, so he also signed a deal with media giant MCA that allowed him to launch his very own label: Doggystyle Records. He started producing other rappers that he found fresh and interesting.

Rap music was now only one part of his whole image. He started auditioning for major roles in movies, a longtime dream. He'd had bit parts before, but with his first starring role in the 2001 horror flick *Bones*, he found that he had some marketable talent. He appeared with Hollywood giant Denzel Washington in the action movie *Training Day* that same year. More and more people started keeping their eyes on his next venture.

This scene from the movie *Training Day* shows actor Denzel Washington as Detective Alonzo Harris talking to Snoop Dogg's character, Blue. Detective Harris is a crooked cop involved in the drug trade, and Blue is a wheelchair-bound drug dealer.

Just Say No

Throughout his career Snoop had depended on others for his success: his wife, his mother, his mentor Dr. Dre. But there was something else that Snoop depended on as well. For most of his teen years and all of his adult life, Snoop has smoked marijuana almost every day. It is an important part of his life that is often featured in his music. Yet as he began to change his image, he was no longer proud of his habit. In *Tha Doggfather* he wrote:

> **"I've got a lifelong habit, a way of getting through the hard times and celebrating the good times that I'm not so sure I could do without and I'm damn sure I wouldn't even want to try. . . . On the other side, I've got two young sons. . . . Am I setting a good example for my sons? If it ever gets to the point where my sons ask me about drugs, I'm going to tell them what I truly feel. They're better off without them. I owe them that much, and if that makes me a hypocrite, then that's just a charge I'll have to cop to."**

In 2002 Snoop said that he was giving up smoking marijuana for the sake of his kids. He needed to be a better role model to them, he told interviewers. But the attraction to drugs was too great. In a 2004 interview with *Rolling Stone*, Snoop admitted that he was smoking marijuana again, although he said he was only using half as much as he had previously.

Going Wild

Not all of Snoop's decisions were made with children in mind. For instance, to further broaden his empire, in 2002 Snoop started an adult film company that produced pornographic videos. He also collaborated with Mantra Films, the makers of the *Girls Gone Wild* series, for *Girls Gone Wild: Doggy Style*. And his own company produced the *Snoop Dogg: Doggystyle* series. Despite the popularity of the videos, Snoop eventually shut down production at the request of his wife.

Some of Snoop's ventures have been unsuccessful, though. Occasionally he hits snags in his efforts to appeal to a wider audience. For instance, in 2002 Snoop agreed to appear as himself in a movie with the Muppets, *A Very Merry Muppet Christmas Movie*. The movie

Snoop Dogg arrives at the premiere of *Soul Plane* with his two sons, Corde and Cordell, also called Spanky and Lil' Snoop. In recent years Snoop Dogg has changed some of his behaviors, in an attempt to set a better example for his sons.

In addition to lending his acting talent to the Muppet movie, Snoop Dogg also appeared, in Muppet-like form, on the Comedy Central program *Crank Yankers*. On the show, puppets act out prank calls for humorous effect.

would mostly be watched by children. A conservative TV personality named Bill O'Reilly protested Snoop's appearance in the Muppet movie asking, "Should a guy who has also been in porn films [and] has a past filled with violence really be appearing in a program designed for little kids?" Snoop responded by saying that the very reason he was appearing was to do something positive for those little kids, but executives were not convinced. After repeated protests by O'Reilly drew more widespread media attention, the movie producers cut Snoop's part.

Snoop Dogg looks out over the crowd as he performs on stage. Snoop is always a commanding presence, and audiences respond. With his new image change, he's become popular with an even bigger audience than before.

6

King of His Crib

Now in his thirties, Snoop is comfortable with success, although being successful doesn't mean that he always makes the right choices. It does mean, however, that he's learned to pick himself up and keep going. And when he does, the world responds with even more support than it had given him before.

One of those poor choices involved his decision to break up with his wife, Shante. In 2004 Snoop filed for divorce, citing irreconcilable differences. However, he soon realized that he was making a mistake, and withdrew the divorce petition. "I said I wanted a divorce, but that ain't really what I wanted," he told *Rolling Stone*'s Erik Hedegaard. "My thing was, I was so demanding and not willing to listen. . . . I just got to come back to being you know, Calvin, and realizing what matters to me most, my wife and kids."

Twenty-First Century Snoop

Snoop continues to walk on the cutting-edge professionally. In 2004 he started his own show on the XM **satellite radio** channel called "Welcome to Da Chuuch with Big Snoop Dogg." The show reflects Snoop's own musical influences. He plays a mixture of 1970s **R&B** and **soul**, as well as more contemporary voices like Too Short, Nas, and Phar Cyde.

Snoop's show was such a success that in December 2005, XM asked him to be the executive producer of their hip-hop channel, The Rhyme. Snoop viewed this as an opportunity to introduce a wider range of music to hip-hop fans. "I am truly excited about being able to have total control over the music and programming for The Rhyme. I will play music that people have never heard and music that they haven't heard in a long time," Snoop told *Rap Weekly* magazine.

Likewise XM views its partnership with Snoop as a significant step in attracting more subscribers. "Snoop is a definitive hip-hop icon," the executive vice president of programming for XM said. "With his new role Snoop will have an even larger platform to bring his unique musical sensibilities to millions of XM listeners."

The Silver Screen

Snoop hasn't forgotten his non-musical interests though. He has said that he is still determined to become a serious movie actor, although he knows he still has a long way to go. "I have a reputation," he said during an interview with *USA Today* reporter Garry Strauss. "The hard part is creating a new reputation. I still make mistakes. I'm not perfect. But I don't claim to be."

Just like everything else in his life, Snoop has gone after his acting goal with determination. He created and starred in his own comedy series on MTV in 2003, *Doggy Fizzle Televizzle*. He also had a small role in the 2004 picture *Starsky and Hutch*, a comedy starring Ben Stiller and Owen Wilson. But by far, Snoop's biggest splash as an actor came in the movie *Soul Plane* in 2004, in which he plays an airplane pilot who is constantly high on marijuana.

The movie spoofs many aspects of African-American culture, such as inner-city living and soul food. But not everyone found it funny. Leah Rozen wrote in *People* magazine that *Soul Plane* "tries to wring laughs from a motley collection of smutty gags and racial stereotypes." But Snoop insisted that the movie was just for laughs. "It's a comedy, not reality," he told interviewer Remy Crane of *Cinema Confidential*. "Its purpose is to make people laugh, to bring people up." Now Snoop

In 2005, Snoop appeared behind a different kind of microphone as host of a channel on XM Radio called The Rhyme. Executives hoped that the rapper's popularity would boost subscription rates to their satellite radio service.

says he is ready for more serious parts. "Now I wanna play roles that are unexpected . . . roles they wrote for a white guy," he said during a 2005 interview with *Blender* magazine.

Coach Snoop

For the last few years, Snoop has been coaching his son Corde's Pop Warner football team, the Rowland Heights Raiders. Snoop has

Coach Snoop Dogg is pictured here with his son's Pop Warner football team, the Rowland Raiders, in December 2003. This photo was taken before a game played as part of a charity event to support the Save a Life Foundation.

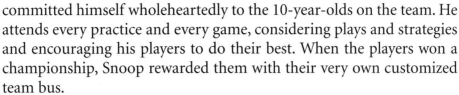

committed himself wholeheartedly to the 10-year-olds on the team. He attends every practice and every game, considering plays and strategies and encouraging his players to do their best. When the players won a championship, Snoop rewarded them with their very own customized team bus.

Devoting himself to helping young people is rewarding for Snoop. "I see how these kids really love me," he told Shaun Robinson of *Access Hollywood.* "They love the person, not Snoop Dogg the rapper, but the person who can actually teach them small things in football that might become big things later on in life." One of his proudest moments came when the Pop Warner football league named him "Coach of the Year" for his dedication to his team.

Snoop even organizes an annual "Snooper Bowl" tournament for the Pop Warner football league, which is held on the day of the actual Super Bowl. The event raises money to support Save-A-Life, Snoop's charitable foundation. Snoop started Save-A-Life in order to help kids growing up in poverty. The foundation supports places like children's hospitals and inner-city youth centers. This recent entry into charitable works has earned him a lot of good credit and publicity.

Snoop Dogg has come to know what is important in life. He has journeyed from the streets of Long Beach to the plushest palaces of Los Angeles. He has partied with celebrities, recorded hit songs, and draped himself in jewels and furs. Snoop has lived extravagantly, but he has never forgotten who and what is truly important: his roots, his friends, his family, and, of course, his music.

1971 Snoop was born Calvin Cordozar Broadus on October 20 in Long Beach, California.

1990 Calvin is convicted of possessing crack cocaine, sentenced to one year in the Wayside Jail in Anaheim, California.

1992 Snoop appears on Dr. Dre's soundtrack for the movie *Deep Cover* on the title track. Dr. Dre and Snoop cut *The Chronic*.

1993 *The Chronic* goes platinum.

Snoop is charged in the killing of Philip Woldemariam.

He releases his debut solo album, *Doggystyle*, produced by Dr. Dre. *Doggystyle* becomes the first debut album in history to hit the music charts at number one, going platinum three times.

1996 Snoop is acquitted of his role in the Woldemariam murder.

Tupac Shakur is killed.

The album *Tha Doggfather* is released.

1997 Snoop marries high school sweetheart, Shante Taylor.

1998 Snoop splits from Death Row Records and signs with No Limit Records.

Da Game Is To Be Sold, Not To Be Told is released.

1999 *Tha Doggfather* is published.

No Limit Top Dogg is released.

2000 Snoop switches from No Limit to MCA.

Snoop Dogg Presents Tha Eastsidaz is released.

The Last Meal is released.

2001 Snoop appears in the horror movie *Bones*.

2002 *Snoop Dogg Presents . . . Doggy Style Allstars Vol. 1* is released.

Paid tha Cost to Be da Bo$$ is released.

2004   Snoop stars in *Soul Plane*.

The XM satellite radio show "Welcome to Da Chuuch with Big Snoop Dogg" debuts.

The Hard Way is released.

R&G (Rhythm & Gangsta): The Masterpiece is released.

2005   Snoop advocates for the release of death row inmate Stanley Tookie, founder of the Crip street gang.

He performs at the Live 8 concert in England to raise awareness of worldwide poverty.

He is also made executive producer of XM satellite radio's hip-hop channel, The Rhyme.

2006   Snoop is arrested at London's Heathrow Airport for his involvement in a riot started by members of his entourage.

Tha Blue Carpet Treatment is released.

Snoop is arrested again in October at Bob Hope Airport in Burbank, California, while parked in a passenger loading zone. Approached by airport security for a traffic infraction, he was found in possession of marijuana and a firearm.

Snoop is sentenced on April 12 to five years of probation for gun and drug charges.

Discography
Albums
1992   *The Chronic*

1993   *Doggystyle*

1996   *Tha Doggfather*

1998   *Da Game Is to Be Sold, Not to Be Told*

1999   *No Limit Top Dogg*

2000   *Snoop Dogg Presents Tha Eastsidaz*
       Tha Last Meal

2002   *Snoop Dogg Presents Doggy Style Allstars Volume 1*
       Paid Tha Cost to Be da Bo$$

2004   *The Hard Way*
       R & G (Rhythm & Gangsta): The Masterpiece

2006   *Tha Blue Carpet Treatment*

Top Ten Singles
1993   "What's My Name?"
       "Gin and Juice"

1998   "Still A G Thang"

1999   "Woof"

2003   "Beautiful"

2004   "Drop It Like It's Hot"

Film Credits
1998   *Half-Baked*
       The Ride

1999   *Hot Boyz*
       Urban Menace

2001   *Baby Boy*
       Training Day
       Bones
       The Wash

2004   *Starsky and Hutch*
       Soul Plane

2005   *Racing Stripes*
        Boss'n Up

2006   *Hood of Horror*
        The Tenants

2007   *Arthur and the Minimoys*
        Coach Snoop

Awards/Honors

1994   *Source* Awards, New Artist of the Year and Lyricist of the Year

        MTV Video Music Awards, Best Rap Video

        Rolling Stone Annual Critics Poll, Best Rapper

1995   American Music Awards, Favorite Rap/Hip-Hop Artist

2002   Adult Video News Awards, Best Music Soundtrack

2003   BET Awards, Best Collaboration

2005   MOBO Awards, Best Video

        MTV Europe Awards, Best Hip-Hop Artist

        Ricky William Foundation/Pop Warner Little Scholars,
            Coach of the Year

        Billboard R&B/Hip-Hop Conference Awards, Hot Rap Track

2006   MTV Australia Video Music Awards, Best Hip-Hop Video

        MTV Video Music Awards, Best Dance Video

        Los Angeles Chapter Recording Academy Honors Recipient

Crane, Remy. "Snoop Dogg of Soul Plane Interview." *Cinema Confidential* (May 25, 2004).

Flick, Larry. "Rap." *Billboard*, May 2, 1992: 84.

Green, Beverly Broadus. *Real Love: The Life of an Extraordinary Woman*. Pittsburgh: RoseDog Books, 2004.

Ordonez, Jennifer. "Rapper Snoop Dogg, the Former Top Dog, Reinvents Himself." *Wall Street Journal*, September 16, 2002.

Rodman, Sarah. "Working Like a Dogg, Inspired By the Late Tupac Shakur and Sobered By His Own Legal Battles, Snoop Is All Business Now." *Boston Herald*, July 4, 1997.

Rozen, Leah. "Soul Plane (Film)." *People* 61, no. 23: 33.

Snoop Dogg, with Davin Seay. *Tha Doggfather: The Times, Trials, and Hardcore Truths of Snoop Dogg*. New York: William Morrow, 1999.

Stossel, Scott. "Gate Crashers." *The New Republic* 221, no. 9: 16-19.

Strauss, Neil. "Snoop Doggy Dogg's New Trick." *Rolling Stone* 793: 45-48.

Tannenbaum Rob. "Hot Dogg." *Blender*, January/February 2005.

Wielenga, Dave. "The Dogg Walks." *Rolling Stone* no. 731: 22-26.

Web Sites

www.allhiphop.com

This website focuses on daily news in the hip-hop world. It frequently features articles on Snoop Dogg's current projects and concerts.

www.rapweekly.com

An online rap and hip-hop magazine features a news archive and daily news and analysis of events in the hip-hop world.

www.rockonthenet.com

A central rock-oriented website has a thorough entry for Snoop, covering all of his awards and nominations, as well as the music chart numbers for all of his albums and singles.

www.snoopdogg.com

Snoop Dogg's official website includes recent news, updates on his current projects, and his tour schedule, as well as biographical information and discography.

www.snoopheaven.com

This general website covers a variety of topics related to Snoop, including a news archive, interviews, and extensive biography.

accomplice—one who aids in a criminal act

acquit—to free or clear from a criminal charge

backlash—a negative reaction to an earlier action

camaraderie—good will between friends

crack cocaine—very strong cocaine that is smoked in a pipe and is highly addictive

evocative—tending to bring out an emotional response

funk—a type of music that combines parts of jazz, blues, and soul

homophobia—irrational fear of gay men and women

impresario—person who sponsors an entertainment event

misogyny—hatred of women

platinum—in the music industry, going platinum means selling 1 million copies

provocative—tending to excite

R&B—rhythm and blues, a type of music that combines blues and jazz

royalties—a share paid to a musician out of the money made from the sale of the musician's work

satellite radio—a radio service sent by satellite to cars, homes, and public places for subscribers who have special equipment that can receive the signal

scrilla—money, specifically cash

soul—a type of music that combines gospel and rhythm and blues

Emma Carlson-Berne has a master's degree in composition and rhetoric from Miami University in Oxford, Ohio, and a bachelor's degree in English from the University of Wisconsin-Madison. She has written or edited several books for middle- and high-school students on different topics, including the history of drugs and the history of suicide. Emma lives in Charleston, South Carolina, with her husband Aaron and her parakeet Avital. She also teaches horseback riding.

Picture Credits